Kids of Character

Bible Study

by
Marilyn Boyer

A character study for children ages 6–12

For use with *Kids of Character Flashcards*

Copyright © 2011 by Marilyn Boyer
ALL RIGHTS RESERVED

Editing & graphic design by Mary Ann Edman

First printing August, 2011

ISBN 978-0-9785859-7-6

Published by The Learning Parent
2430 Sunnymeade Road
Rustburg, VA 24588
www.thelearningparent.com

Proudly printed in the United States of America by Jostens

KIDS OF CHARACTER

BIBLE STUDY

This book belongs to

Instructions for Use

This study is intended to be used in coordination with *Kids of Character Flashcards*. In order to implement character in their lives, children must first know what it is and how to apply it. That is the purpose of this study. You can work through this study at your own rate doing as few as two or three questions a day, or more if desired.

While working through the Scripture study, work on the corresponding flashcard each day until the verse and definition are learned.

When you move on to the next quality in your study, continue reviewing flashcards previously learned as well as learning the new quality.

At the end of the study, take a few more days to review any verses and definitions you still have trouble saying, until all are learned well.

NOTE TO PARENTS: If you are doing this study with multiple ages, you can read the question aloud to those not able to read.

Table of Contents

Alertness 9
Attentiveness 13
Availability 17
Boldness 21
Compassion 25
Contentment 29
Courage 33
Decisiveness 37
Deference 41
Dependability 45
Diligence 49
Discernment 53
Discretion 57
Endurance 61
Enthusiasm 65
Flexibility 69
Forgiveness 73
Generosity 77
Gentleness 81
Gratefulness 85
Honesty 89
Honor 93

Hospitality ... 97
Humility ... 101
Initiative ... 105
Joyfulness ... 109
Kindness ... 113
Love ... 117
Loyalty ... 121
Meekness ... 125
Obedience ... 129
Orderliness ... 133
Patience ... 137
Persuasiveness ... 141
Prudence ... 145
Punctuality ... 149
Resourcefulness ... 153
Respectfulness ... 157
Self-Control ... 161
Sensitivity ... 165
Thoroughness ... 169
Tolerance ... 173
Truthfulness ... 177
Virtue ... 181
Wisdom ... 185
Additional Resources ... 188

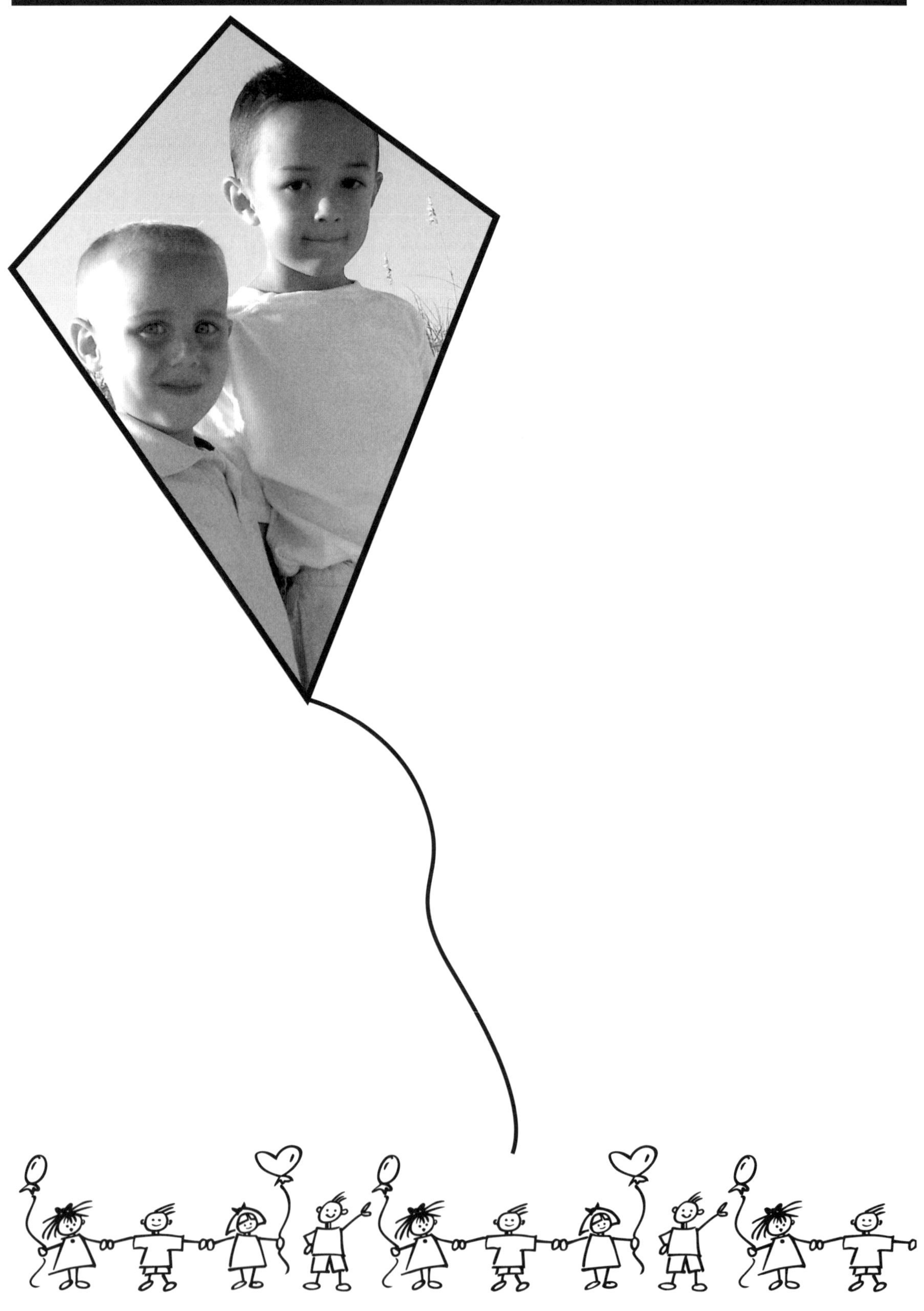

ALERTNESS

DEFINITION

Being keenly aware of what is taking place around me so I can be prepared with a right response

MEMORY VERSE

Be sober, be vigilant; because your adversary the devil,
as a roaring lion, walketh about,
seeking whom he may devour.

I Peter 5:8

1. Who will always be opposed to God and His purposes?

____

2. Should we be surprised when others don't share our values?

____

3. If we are actively doing right, will others oppose us?

____

The Bible uses the word "watchful" for alertness.

Colossians 4:6

1. How should we be ready to share with others?

Luke 12:37

1. Who is called blessed in this verse?

2. Why?

Luke 21:26

1. We are on this earth for God's purposes. How does this verse tell us to be prepared?

APPLICATION

IF'S

1. You are in a restaurant and listen as your dad shares the gospel with another customer. You realize you would not be able to communicate how to be saved effectively if someone asked you. What should you do?

____

____

____

____

2. You are watching your little brother at the park. You notice a strange looking man who keeps staring at your brother. What should you do?

____

____

____

____

3. Your two-year-old sister is twirling around the room singing, holding an American flag. You notice the sharp point on the end of the flag. What should you do?

____

____

____

____

4. On family night in church people have begun calling out on someone to share a Bible verse recently learned. What should you do before family night this week?

____

____

____

____

ATTENTIVENESS

DEFINITION

Listening with the ears, eyes, and heart

MEMORY VERSE

The ear that heareth the reproof of life
abideth among the wise.

Proverbs 15:31

Proverbs 20:12

"The hearing ________________ and the seeing ________________,
the Lord hath ______________________ both of them."

1. What does this verse tell you to do that shows you are learning wisdom?

____

____

God made our eyes and ears to be used for His purposes.

Proverbs 4:20-21

1. What does Solomon tell his son to do?

Attend ____

Incline ____

Let them not ____

Keep them ____

This shows we can be responsible to listen attentively.

1 Samuel 3:10

1. Who is a good example of attentiveness in this passage?

____

____

1 Samuel 3:19

2. What does this verse tell us about whether or not Samuel paid attention to what he heard? ____

____

____

Proverbs 23:26

1. "My son, ________ me thine _______ and let thine ____________ observe my ways."

2. Can we control the use of our eyes and heart?

____

APPLICATION

IF'S

1. If your dad is explaining to you how to do a math problem, but you're thinking about hunting, are you being attentive? What should you do?

2. If you are in church and the pastor is preaching, are you being attentive if you are whispering to your sister? What should you do?

3. If your mom is giving you instructions because she has to go run errands, but you're thinking about how to get your puzzle together, are you being attentive? What should you do? What do the words "focus" and "concentrate" mean?

4. If your little brother is telling you about a dream he had but you keep on reading your book, are you being attentive? Why not? What should you do?

AVAILABILITY

DEFINITION

Being willing to attend to a need when I am called to help

MEMORY VERSE

Also I heard the voice of the Lord, saying, Whom shall I send, and who will go for us? Then said I, Here am I; send me.

Isaiah 6:8

1. What was Isaiah willing to do?

____

____

2. What should be our response when we feel God wants us to do something?

____

____

I Samuel 3

1. What was Samuel willing to do?

____

____

2. Did he make excuses?

____

____

3. Did he question God's judgment?

4. Did God bless him for it?

APPLICATION

IF'S

1. In church there is a family whose Dad just had back surgery. It snowed last night and they need their driveway shoveled so he can go to the doctor. What should you do?

____

____

____

____

2. The church is looking for families to volunteer at the Salvation Army church service. They need a piano player. You are a great piano player. What should you do?

____

____

____

____

Boldness

DEFINITION

Facing confrontation with the assurance that God will bless the outcome if I'm standing firm for truth

MEMORY VERSE

The rich man is wise in his own conceit; but the poor that hath understanding searcheth him out.

Proverbs 28:11

1. Where does true boldness come from?

____

____

II Corinthians 10:1-2

1. Why was Paul bold in this passage?

____

____

I Thessalonians 2:2

1. What purpose gave them boldness?

____

____

Philippians 1:14

1. What helped to give boldness for the Philippian believers?

Hebrews 4:16

1. How should we approach the throne of grace?

APPLICATION

IF'S

1. You are at a homeschool function where the kids are watching a movie while the parents meet. You realize the DVD is something your parents wouldn't want you to watch. Your four younger brothers and sisters are there with you. What should you do?

____

____

____

____

2. You feel impressed to share the Gospel with the widow lady next door. What should you do?

____

____

____

____

COMPASSION

DEFINITION

Being willing to expend effort to help alleviate the suffering of those in need

MEMORY VERSE

Withhold not good from them to whom it is due,
when it is in the power of thine hand to do it.
Say not to thy neighbor, Go, and come again,
and tomorrow I will give; when thou hast it by thee.
Proverbs 3:27-28

1. If your neighbor is in need and you have the means to help, what does this verse tell you to do?

____

____

2. What does verse it say about putting them off or telling them to come later?

____

____

____

____

Proverbs 12:10

1. What does this verse tell us about caring for our pets?

____

____

I Peter 3:8

1. What does this verse say about compassion?

____

____

Mark 5:19

1. Who had compassion on us?

____

APPLICATION

IF'S

1. You find a stray kitten with a broken back. What should you do?

2. In church there is a little girl with Down's Syndrome. She loves talking to people, but others seem scared to be around her. What should you do?

CONTENTMENT

DEFINITION

Realizing that God has given me all I need
for my present happiness

MEMORY VERSE

Not that I speak in respect of want: for I have learned,
in whatsoever state I am, therewith to be content.
I know how to be abased, and I know how to abound:
everywhere and in all things I am instructed both to be full
and to be hungry, both to abound and to suffer need.

Philippians 4:11-12

1. What had Paul learned?

____

____

2. Does Paul's spirit depend on material provision?

____

____

I Timothy 6:6

1. What is great gain?

____

____

Hebrews 13:5

1. How are we instructed in this verse?

____

____

____

____

APPLICATION

IF'S

1. You left your bike behind the car. Dad didn't see it and rode over it. You are disappointed of course. What should you remember?

____

____

____

____

2. Dad's work is very slow right now. You usually get to choose your birthday dinner, but not this year. You're having spaghetti instead of steak. What attitude should you have?

____

____

____

____

COURAGE

DEFINITION

Standing alone for righteousness and yielding my fears to God

MEMORY VERSE

Have not I commanded thee? Be strong and of a good courage; be not afraid, neither be thou dismayed; for the Lord thy God is with thee whithersoever thou goest.

Joshua 1:9

1. What does God command Joshua? "Be ______________________ and of a good ______________________; be not __________________, neither be thou ____________________."

2. Why does he tell him not be afraid?

____

____

Courage is doing what God tells us to do regardless of how we feel, realizing God is in control.

II Chronicles 32 tells us the account of a man named Hezekiah who was a king of Judah. The army from Assyria was coming against them in battle. Read how Hezekiah encouraged his people prior to the battle.

II Chronicles 32:7-8 (Fill in the blanks): "Be ______________ and __________________,
be not __________________ nor ____________________ for the King of Assyria, nor
for all the ___________________ that is with him; for there be ____________________
with us than with _____________________. With him is an ____________________ of
_____________________; but with us is the ______________ our _________________
to __________________ us, and to __________________ our ___________________."

It says the people rested themselves upon the words of Hezekiah. What he told them sounds much like what God told _______________________________ in Joshua 1.

We will find one more example. See how similar were David's words to his son Solomon.
I Chronicles 28:20 "Be _________________ and of ___________ _________________,
and ____________ it: _________________ not, nor be ________________: for the Lord
_________________ even ________ ________________, will be with ____________."

1. Why should we not be afraid if God calls us to do something for Him?

____

____

APPLICATION

IF'S

1. You are called upon in church to quote a Bible verse you just learned. You are scared to talk in front of people. What should you do?

2. You are at a friend's house and he tells you, "Hey, come watch this TV program with me. It's a good one. Your mom won't mind." You know your mom and dad told you not to watch anything without permission from them. What should you do?

3. You are with a friend and he is about to pick the neighbor's raspberries without permission. He wants you to join him. What should you do?

4. You are afraid of dogs. Dad asked you to walk next door and check on Mr. Edwards, who is at home with a broken leg. His dog runs up to you as you approach his door. What should you do?

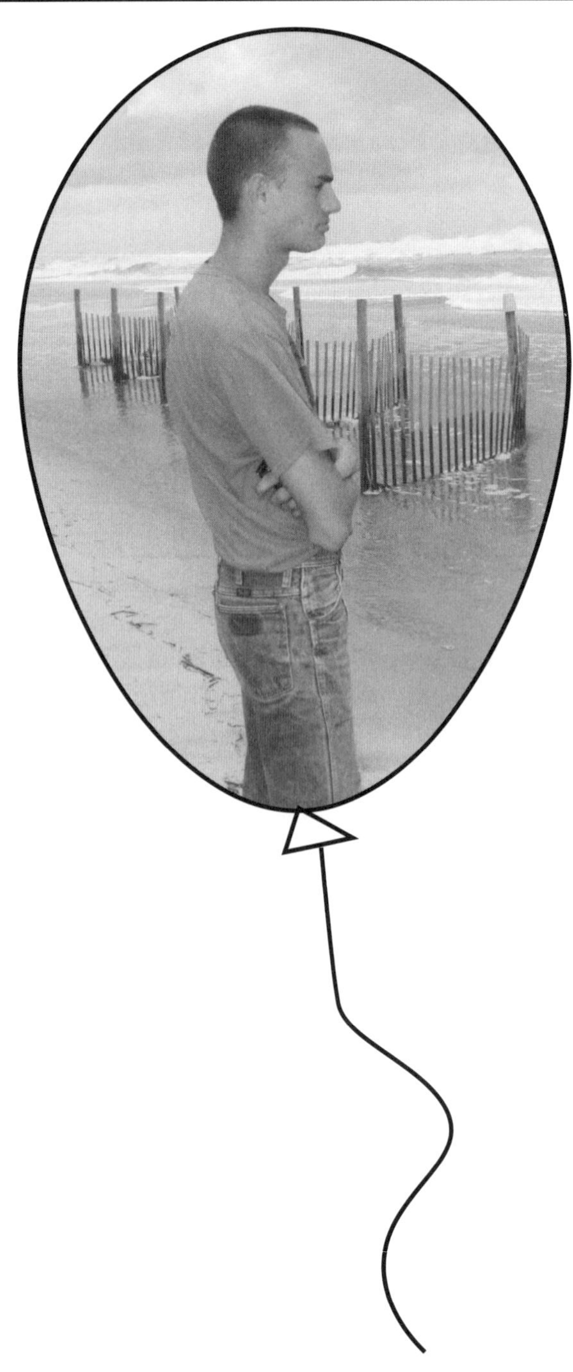

DECISIVENESS

DECISIVENESS

DEFINITION

The ability to make wise, deliberate decisions based on God's standards

MEMORY VERSE

But let him ask in faith, nothing wavering. For he that doubts is like a wave of the sea, driven with the wind and tossed.

James 1:6

1. What in nature is one who is indecisive compared to?

____

____

2. What does verse 8 tell us about a double-minded man?

____

____

James 4:8

1. What instruction is given to an indecisive man?

____

____

Hebrews 10:23 (Fill in the blanks): "Let us ______________ ________________ the

_________________ of our _______________ without ____________________.

(For he ______ ____________________ that _______________________.")

Proverbs 9:10

1. What is the beginning of wisdom?

____

2. What are wise decisions based on?

____

APPLICATION

IF'S

1. A friend invites you to his house to watch a movie. What should you do?

2. You're at a friend's house. They want to spend the afternoon playing computer games. You'd like to do something else. What should you do?

3. You hear of an elderly man at church who is recovering from surgery. You wonder if there are things he might need done around his home. What should you do?

DEFERENCE

DEFINITION

To hold others in esteem and give them first choice

MEMORY VERSE

Let nothing be done through strife or vainglory; but in lowliness of mind let each esteem other better than themselves.

Philippians 2:3

1. How are we to treat others?

____

____

2. When we do this, what quality are we demonstrating?

____

Proverbs 11:25

"Liberal" in this verse means "generous." What will be the outcome for the one who chooses to be generous?

I Peter 5:5

"Indeed all of you should defer one to another and wear the overalls of humility in serving one another." –(TLB)

"Be clothed with humility." –(KJV)

This verse implies that we must take the initiative to "put on" humility and defer to one another. It doesn't just happen. We must purposely choose to exercise humility.

1. What is our duty to other people?

____

____

2. What is our part in being sure this happens?

____

____

APPLICATION

IF'S

1. Your family is having friends over for the evening. You were planning on playing Bible trivia, but their kids want to draw pictures. What should you do?

____

____

____

____

2. You are taking your sister out to lunch for her birthday. Where should you take her?

____

____

____

____

3. You'd been planning all week to go fishing on Saturday. Your little sister has been sick all week and on Saturday she REALLY wanted to go to the museum. What should you do?

____

____

____

____

DEPENDABILITY

DEFINITION

Honoring your word and responsibilities even if it means unexpected sacrifice

MEMORY VERSE

He sweareth to his own hurt, and changeth not.

Psalm 15:4b

This verse is talking about who shall abide in God's holy hill.

1. What happens if you agreed to do something, but unexpected difficulties cropped up? Should you still attempt to keep your word?

____

____

____

____

2. What does God honor?

____

____

____

____

"Steadfast" is a word Scripture uses for dependability.

I Corinthians 15:58

1. What does this verse tell us to demonstrate in our work for the Lord?

____

____

____

____

APPLICATION

IF'S

1. You were invited to a friend's birthday party. Their mom asked you to bring your mom's special no-bake cookies. Your mom isn't feeling well on the day of the party. What should you do?

____

____

____

____

2 Mom had to take your brother to the dentist. She told you to remember to turn the oven on at 4:00 so that dinner would be ready on time. You're afraid you'll forget. What should you do?

____

____

____

____

BLAZE and the
LOST QUARRY

DILIGENCE

DEFINITION

Viewing each task given to me as a special duty and putting forth the effort to do my very best

MEMORY VERSE

And whatsoever you do in word or deed, do all in the name of the Lord Jesus, giving thanks to God and the Father by him.

Colossians 3:17

1. Why should we do our best at whatever we do?

____

____

____

____

Proverbs 12:24

1. How will God bless the diligent?

____

____

____

____

Proverbs 27:23

1. What are your "flocks and herds"—what things are you responsible for?

APPLICATION

IF'S

1. Your job is to unload the dishwasher. As you remove some of the dishes, you discover they are still wet. What should you do?

____

____

____

____

2. It's Monday morning. You know dusting is your chore for Monday. What should you do?

____

____

____

____

DISCERNMENT

DEFINITION

The ability to identify subtle untruths or motives

MEMORY VERSE

For the word of God is quick, powerful, and sharper than any two-edged sword, piercing even to the dividing asunder of soul and spirit, and of the joints and marrow, and is a discerner of the thoughts and intents of the heart.

Hebrews 4:12

1. What will build discernment in our spirit?

____

____

____

____

2. What does the Word of God do?

____

____

____

____

3. Can the Word of God help us to discern our own hearts?

I Kings 3:9

1. For what did Solomon ask God?

I Corinthians 2:14

1. What does an unsaved man think of the things of the Spirit of God?

2. Who can discern such things?

3. Why?

Proverbs 7:7

1. Can we discern the character of another person?

APPLICATION

IF'S

1. You are reading a book you got from the library. It is all about monkeys and is very interesting. You get to a part that states that man developed from monkeys. What should you do?

____

____

____

____

2. You are outside shooting baskets when one of the big boys in the neighborhood comes over and starts praising your basketball skills. Then he asks if he can borrow your dad's new riding lawn mower. What should you do?

____

____

____

____

3. You are at a friend's house and the T.V. is on. You see inappropriate behavior being shown. What should you do?

____

____

____

____

Discretion

DEFINITION

Avoiding any words, actions, or attitudes that could give the appearance of evil

MEMORY VERSE

The proverbs of Solomon the son of David, king of Israel … to give subtlety to the simple, to the young man knowledge and discretion.

Proverbs 1:1, 4

1. Why were the Proverbs written?

____

____

____

____

2. What would they teach the young man?

____

____

____

____

Titus 2:5

1. What are older women to teach the younger women?

Proverbs 11:22

1. To what is a pretty woman who is without discretion compared?

Proverbs 2:11

1. What will guard you?

Proverbs 19:11

1. What will help you to control your anger?

APPLICATION

IF'S

1. A boy in church is making up words that rhyme with bad words and using them in place of bad words. What should you do?

____

____

____

____

2. Your buddy is rolling up paper and making "cigarettes" to make people think he's smoking. What should you do?

____

____

____

____

3. Your friend always wants to lock the door when you're playing in your room. What should you do?

____

____

____

____

We always had the rule that you're never to pretend to be doing wrong. Also, never allow yourself to be in a position where another person might conclude you were involved in wrong doing.

ENDURANCE

DEFINITION

The inward struggle to endure tribulation with determination

MEMORY VERSE

For what glory is it, if, when ye be buffeted for your faults, ye shall take it patiently? But if, when ye do well, and suffer for it, ye take it patiently, this is acceptable with God.

I Peter 2:20

1. Do we get a reward if we suffer deservingly?

____

2. What example did Christ leave us?

____

____

3. What do we learn through suffering unjustly?

____

____

Philippians 4:5

1. What should we strive to put into practice?

I Peter 2:19-20

1. What is thankworthy?

2. What is acceptable to God?

Hebrews 6:15

1. How did Abraham endure?

I Timothy 2:3

1. What is a characteristic of a good soldier?

APPLICATION

IF'S

1. Mom needs water brought from the neighbor's house. It's hot and sticky inside and the babies are fussy. Mom is expecting another baby. What should you do?

____

____

____

____

2. You were expecting to get your braces off today. The orthodontist tells you it will be three more months. What should you do?

____

____

____

____

ENTHUSIASM

DEFINITION

Expressing joy in each job I am given to do

MEMORY VERSE

And whatsoever you do, do it heartily as to the Lord, and not unto men.

Colossians 3:23

1. When we do a job, who are we actually serving?

____

2. What kind of effort should we give a task we're assigned to?

____

3. Would you have a different attitude about doing a job you didn't want to do if you thought about God watching you? Look up this verse: Genesis 16:13. Who does it say is watching us?

____

It's a good verse to remember every day.

II Chronicles 16:9

1. What does this verse tell us?

____

2. Is God always watching you?

____

Philippians 4:4

1. What does this verse say about our attitude?

____

____

____

APPLICATION

IF'S

1. If you follow an instruction Mom gives you, but you have a whining attitude, did you really obey?

2. Mom says it's spring cleaning day. Everyone has extra chores and less than usual school work. You feel like whining, but what should you do?

3. Your little brother was told to clean up the yard. He is fussing, walking slowly, and crying. How can you teach him to have enthusiasm?

FLEXIBILITY

DEFINITION

Cheerfully being willing to change my plans when circumstances beyond my control require it

MEMORY VERSE

Be anxious for nothing; but in everything by prayer and supplication with thanksgiving, let your requests be made known unto God. And the peace of God, which passeth all understanding, shall guard your hearts and minds through Christ Jesus.

Philippians 4:6-7

I Corinthians 9:19-23

1. Why was Paul willing to be flexible in this passage?

Proverbs 16:9

1. We are told to make our plans, but who is it that orders our steps?

2. If God changes our plans, what should be our response?

Jeremiah 10:23

1. What should be our expectation concerning our plans?

Philippians 4: 6, 7

1. What should be our response if our plans do change unexpectedly?

2. When will God give us peace?

APPLICATION

IF'S

1. You had been planning on spending the afternoon reading in the tree house. Mom just harvested three bushels of beans from the garden that she needs to can. What should you do?

2. Dad had promised a family trip to Gettysburg this weekend, but Dad and two sisters wake up sick today. What should your attitude be? Also, what could you do to help your sisters pass the time?

FORGIVENESS

DEFINITION

Picturing how Jesus died on the cross for my sins so that God's love can flow through me to others who have wronged me

MEMORY VERSE

Forbearing one another, and forgiving one another,
if any man have a quarrel against any:
even as Christ forgave you, so also do ye.
Colossians 3:13

1. Must we always forgive those who wrong us?

____

2. Why must we do this?

____

____

____

____

Matthew 18:21

1. Peter asked Jesus how often he should forgive his brother. What was Jesus' answer?

Luke 6:37

1. What must we do to be forgiven?

Matthew 6:12

1. What does the Lord's Prayer tell us concerning forgiveness?

APPLICATION

IF'S

1. Dad promised to take you fishing today, but he got up early and went to his office, totally forgetting your plans. What should you do?

____

____

____

____

2. A man in church mistook you for a boy/girl causing trouble and told your dad. Dad believes you, but now what should you do?

____

____

____

____

3. Your baby sister grabbed your Bible and tore out several pages while you were out of the room. What should you do?

____

____

____

____

GENEROSITY

DEFINITION

Giving unselfishly to the needs of others

MEMORY VERSE

Give, and it shall be given unto you; good measure, pressed down, and shaken together, and running over, shall men give into your bosom. For with the same measure that ye mete withal it shall be measured to you again.

Luke 6:38

1. How will God bless true generosity?

____

____

____

____

Proverbs 22:9

1. Who will receive God's blessing?

____

Why?

____

____

Proverbs 11:25 (A word used for "generous" is "liberal.")

1. What will be the reward for the generous man?

Matthew 5:42

1. What were Jesus' words concerning others in need?

APPLICATION

IF'S

1. You get five candy bars for your birthday. Your little brother is looking longingly at them. What should you do?

2. You hear of a family who has a little girl with leukemia. It's Christmastime and they are so busy taking care of their little girl, they haven't thought about Christmas shopping. What can you do?

3. You know a widow in your church. What might you do to encourage her?

GENTLENESS

GENTLENESS

DEFINITION

Responding to others in a kind, understanding manner

MEMORY VERSE

And the servant of the Lord must not strive;
but be gentle unto all men, apt to teach, patient.
2 Timothy 2:24

List the fruit of the Spirit *(Galatians 5:22-23)*:

"But the fruit of the Spirit is

________________, ________________,

________________, ________________,

________________, ________________,

________________, ________________,

________________; against such there is no law."

1. What number in the list is gentleness?

____

2 Timothy 2:24-25

List the character qualities of a servant of the Lord:

____

____

____

____

____

Titus 3:3

"To speak ____________ of no man, to be no ______________, but ____________, shewing ____________ unto __________ men."

I Thessalonians 2:7

1. What was Paul's attitude toward the Thessalonians?

____

____

2. What relationship did he point out to illustrate it?

____

____

____

____

GENTLENESS

APPLICATION

IF'S

1. Your little brother accidentally knocked over your block castle. What should you do?

____

____

____

____

2. Your baby sister has colic and you are growing so weary of hearing her cry. What should you do?

____

____

____

____

3. You're trying to help your brother with his math problems. It seems like he just can't get it. What should you do?

____

____

____

____

GRATEFULNESS

DEFINITION

Realizing God has given me all I need and
being appreciative to God and others

MEMORY VERSE

Giving thanks always for all things unto God and the Father
in the name of our Lord Jesus Christ.
Ephesians 5:20

1. Which things are we to be thankful for?

____

2. How often should we give thanks?

____

Philippians 4:6 (Fill in the blanks):

"Be ____________________ for ____________________;
but in ____________________ by ____________________
and ____________________ with ____________________
let your ____________________ be made known unto ____________________."

"Careful" in this verse means to become distracted or anxious. This verse cautions us about being distracted by circumstances.

1. When we pray to God we may ask Him for things, but what should we include with our requests?

___

2. For what should we give thanks?

___

I Thessalonians 5:18

1. For what are we to be thankful?

___

2. Why?

___

___

___

___

APPLICATION

IF'S

1. You were planning to go on a family picnic at the lake. When you wake up, it's raining. What should you do?

2. Mom has been working in the kitchen all afternoon to fix a nice dinner. What should you remember to do?

3. You win a gold cup at your piano recital this year. Everyone is congratulating you. Remembering that Dad has paid for your lessons and Mom has taken her time to take you each week to lessons, what should you do?

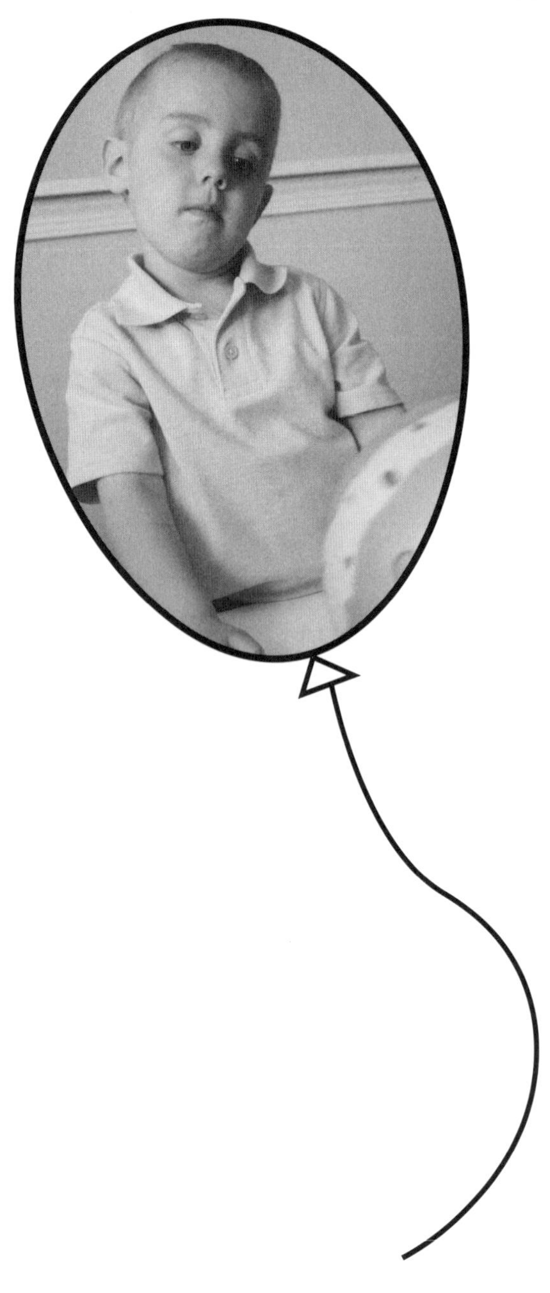

HONESTY

DEFINITION

Speaking the truth in all situations

MEMORY VERSE

Lie not one to another, seeing that ye have put off the old man with his deeds.

Colossians 3:9

1. Is it right to tell "white lies"?

____

2. Is it okay to lie and then say you were joking?

____

Proverbs 12:22

1. What is an abomination to God?

____

____

____

2. What delights God?

____

____

____

Proverbs 16:13

1. What delights those in authority?

____

____

____

I Timothy 2:2

1. What are we to pray for for all men?

____

____

____

I Thessalonians 4:11-12

1. What are you to learn to do? Fill in the blanks:

"And that ye ______________ to be ____________________, and to do
your _________ ____________________, and to ________________
with your _____________ ______________, as we commanded you, that
ye may ________________ ____________________ toward them that are
without, and that ye may have ______________ of ____________________."

2. What is an example to those who are "without" (non-Christians)?

____

____

____

APPLICATION

IF'S

1. You just stepped on the cat's bowl of milk and spilled it. You could just let Mom think the cat did it. What should you do?

____

____

____

____

2. You were playing softball. You accidentally broke the neighbor's window. What should you do?

____

____

____

____

HONOR

DEFINITION

Viewing and treating others as a special creation of God

MEMORY VERSE

Honor all men. Love the brotherhood.
Fear God. Honor the king.

I Peter 2:17

1. This verse tells us to:

Honor ___________ ______________________________

Love _____________ ______________________________

Fear ______________________________

Honor __________ ________________________________

I Timothy 5:17-18

1. To whom shall we give double honor?

____

____

2. Why?

____

____

____

Ephesians 2:10

1. "For we are his ______________________, created in ____________ ______________." If this is true, how should we treat God's workmanship?

____

____

____

____

Exodus 20:12

1. How are you to treat your father and mother?

____

2. Why?

____

____

____

____

Romans 12: 10

1. "We are to be ____________ ______________________ one to another with ______________ ____________; in ____________ preferring one another."

To prefer another means to put the other person before ourselves.

APPLICATION

IF'S

1. If a family comes over for dinner and they have a child about the same age as you, and he wants to play *Candy Land,* but you want to play *Life,* what should you do?

____

____

____

____

2. If Dad begins speaking to you while you are reading a book, how can you show him honor?

____

____

____

____

3. If your little brother goes into a long explanation telling you something he's just learned, but you already know and you're really bored, what should you do?

____

____

____

____

4. If you are about to open the door to walk into a store with your mom, how can you show her honor?

____

____

____

____

HOSPITALITY

DEFINITION

Making those who visit our home feel comfortable

MEMORY VERSE

...Given to hospitality

Romans 12:13b

1. What does this verse tell us we should be "given to"?

____

Hebrews 13:2 (Fill in the blanks):

"Be not __________________ to ______________________________:

for thereby some have entertained __________________________ unawares."

1. Should we as a family invite folks into our home?

____

At our house, when we had other families over, I would "assign" each one of my children to one of the visiting children. In this way they could be certain the child they were assigned to didn't get excluded, that they had someone to talk to, that someone would ask them what they would like to do, etc.

2. What could you determine to do when you have guests in your home?

1 Peter 4:9

1. What does this verse tell us to do?

2. What attitude does it warn us against?

Titus 1:8

1. What responsibility does a person in church leadership have concerning hospitality?

APPLICATION

IF'S

1. Your family is inviting another family over for dinner. You have six children in your family. The family coming over has four. What can you do to show hospitality?

2. A missionary family is on furlough. Their children are lonely and timid. What can you suggest to your parents to be hospitable to them?

3. Your family is ministering to an unsaved family. What can you do to be hospitable?

HUMILITY

DEFINITION

Acknowledging that any good I have achieved is a gift from God, and my life is to be used as an instrument in His hand

MEMORY VERSE

He hath shown thee, O man, what is good; and what doth the Lord require of thee, but to do justly, and to love mercy, and to walk humbly with thy God?

Micah 6:8

1. What does God require of us?

____

____

____

____

I Peter 5:6

1. What are we to do?

____

____

2. What will God do in His time?

____

____

James 4:10

1. What are we told to do?

____

____

2. What will God's response be?

____

____

Acts 20:19

1. How should we serve the Lord?

____

____

APPLICATION

IF'S

1. People are praising you for your musical talent. What should you do?

2. You are getting complimented on your naturally curly hair. What should you say?

INITIATIVE

DEFINITION

Seeing a need and taking responsibility to meet it without being asked

MEMORY VERSE

Whatsoever thy hand findeth to do, do it with thy might.

Ecclesiastes 9:10a

1. Should we look for things to do to be helpful?

___

Ephesians 2:10:

"For we are his workmanship, created in Christ Jesus unto good works, which God hath before ordained that we should walk in them."

1. For what were we created?

___

2. Should we try to avoid work?

___

3. Is work good for us?

___

Luke 17:10

This verse talks about duty. There are things we are responsible to do. Initiative is going beyond, seeing a need and meeting it without being told to. This is being a profitable servant of God.

1. What do you think would be your mom's response if you began using initiative?

____

____

____

2. How do you think you would feel if you begin demonstrating initiative?

____

____

____

APPLICATION

IF'S

1. You walk into the kitchen and notice a wrapper the dog has pulled out of the trash and left on the floor. What should you do?

____

____

____

____

2. Mom is fixing dinner. The baby begins to cry and needs to be fed. Mom goes to attend to the baby. You notice she left in the middle of grating cheese for dinner. What should you do?

____

____

____

____

3. Your little brother just finished his snack. His hands are messy and he got crumbs on the chair and on the floor. What should you do?

____

____

____

____

JOYFULNESS

JOYFULNESS

DEFINITION

Choosing to have a good attitude even when circumstances are tough to bear

MEMORY VERSE

Rejoice in the Lord always; and again I say, Rejoice.

Philippians 4:4

1. This verse tells us to rejoice ______________________________.

Rejoice means to be glad, to have joy in. To be joyful doesn't necessarily mean happy. We can be joyful even in a rough situation. Joy is from deep within; a trust in knowing God has ordained what is best for me. Happiness is more temporary; joy springs from a deep trust in God.

II Corinthians 6:10a:

Paul is instructing others to see themselves as ministers of God even in tough circumstances. Fill in the blanks:

"As ________________________, yet ____________________

_________________________;"

I Thessalonians 5:16:

Write this short verse. "______________ ________________."

James 1:2

1. What does this verse tell us to do when we fall into various trials?

____

____

Colossians 1:10-11

1. This verse admonishes us to walk worthy of the Lord. For verse 11, fill in the blanks:

"Strengthened with all might, according to his ______________ ______________,

unto all ______________________ and ______________________________ with

______________________________."

Notice we are to be joyful even while undergoing trials.

APPLICATION

IF'S

1. You were all excited about going to the science museum today. You woke up sick and will have to spend your day in bed. What should you do?

____

____

____

____

2. Mom's dad is in the hospital. She is traveling to be with him and will be gone for several days. Your siblings are very sad and aren't too comfortable with the babysitter who will be in charge while Dad's at work. What should you do?

____

____

____

____

KINDNESS

DEFINITION

Treating others as you would like to be treated by them

MEMORY VERSE

And be ye kind one to another, tenderhearted, forgiving one another, even as God for Christ's sake hath forgiven you.

Ephesians 4:32

1. What are two descriptions of kindness found in this verse?

____

____

2. Why should we forgive others?

____

____

3. What do you think "tenderhearted" means?

____

____

4. Name a person you know who is kind and tenderhearted toward you.

____

II Peter 1: 5-7

1. This is a list of things we are to add to our faith. List them:

Add to your faith ____;

Add to virtue ____;

Add to knowledge ____;

Add to temperance _______________________________________;

Add to patience ____;

Add to godliness _____________________ ________________________;

Add to brotherly kindness _____________.

2. Circle kindness on the list.

Colossians 3:12-13

This is another list of things we are to "put on." To "put on" shows that we are responsible to do something about it. We should take the initiative for Christ's sake. Fill in the blanks: "Put on therefore, as the elect of God, holy and beloved, bowels of ____________________, _________________________________, _________________________________ of mind, _________________________, _________________________, forbearing one another, and ___________________________ one another."

Proverbs 31:26

1. What is a characteristic of the words of the virtuous woman?

____

Proverbs 19:22

1. What does this verse say will make others like you?

____

2. Do you prefer to be around a kind person or a crabby, selfish person?

____

3. How do others see you?

____

APPLICATION

IF'S

1. Your little brother spilled his orange juice and is crying. What should you do?

2. You are making a complicated Lego creation. Your little sister is watching you longingly. What can you do that would be kind to her without destroying your building?

3. Your friend borrowed your favorite book and left it out in the rain. What should you do?

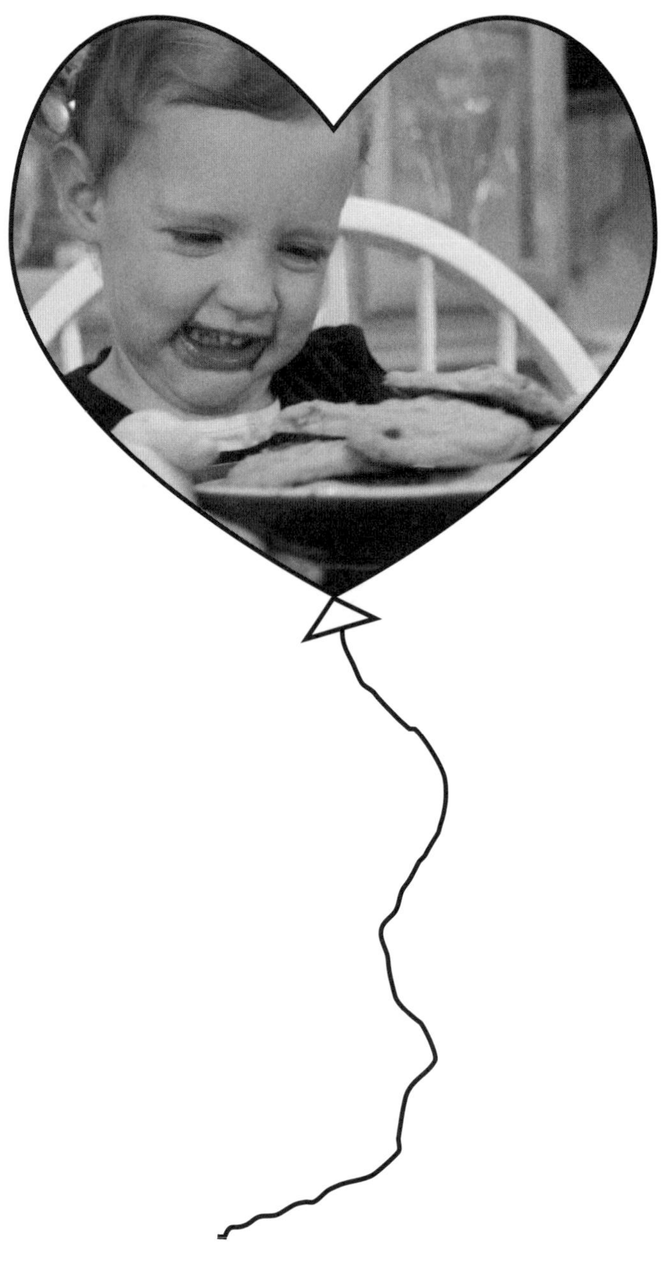

LOVE

DEFINITION

Giving unselfishly in all situations

MEMORY VERSE

Little children, let us not love in word, neither in tongue; but in deed and in truth.

I John 3:18

1. How do we prove we have love? *(Ephesians 5:2)*

____

____

I John 4:20

1. Do we really love God if we hate another person?

____

John 15:13

1. What does this verse tell us?

____

____

____

2. How could you “lay down” your life for others—not die, but giving up your own desires?

___

___

___

I John 4:10-11

1. What is love?

___

___

___

2. Why should we love one another?

___

___

___

APPLICATION

IF'S

1. You've been saving for a new bicycle. You've almost got enough money. You hear of a family with four children who lost their home in a fire. God prompts you to want to do something. What should you do?

____

____

____

____

2. You are at a homeschool Christmas party. You win the Scripture memory game and get first pick of all the prizes. You'd really like the MP3 player, but you see a baby doll that you know your little sister would love. What should you do?

____

____

____

____

LOYALTY

DEFINITION

Committed to the welfare of those I serve,
even to the detriment of my own comfort

MEMORY VERSE

Most men will proclaim their own goodness;
but a faithful man who can find?
Proverbs 20:6

A word for used for "loyal" in Scripture is "faithful."

Proverbs 13:17

1. What is a faithful ambassador?

___

Proverbs 14:5

1. Will a loyal messenger lie?

___

Proverbs 20:6

1. Are faithful men plentiful?

___

Psalm 31:23

1. What will God do for the faithful?

Nehemiah 7:2

1. What type of man was Nehemiah?

Luke 16:10

1. What is said of one who is faithful in little matters?

APPLICATION

IF'S

1. Some kids at church are talking meanly about your little brother. What should you do?

2. You promised your sister you'd take a walk with her. Your friend calls and wants you to go for ice cream. What should you do?

Meekness

DEFINITION

Yielding my expectations (rights) to God
without getting angry

MEMORY VERSE

The meek will he guide in judgment:
and the meek will he teach his way.
Psalm 25:9

Matthew 5:5

1. What does this verse say of the meek?

___

I Peter 3:4

1. What are 2 qualities that a woman should seek?

___

___

Matthew 11:29

1. What does this verse say of Jesus' character?

___

___

Galatians 5:23

1. List the qualities that are fruits of the Spirit:

____

____

____

____

____

____

____

____

____

Colossians 3:12

1. What are we to "put on"?

____

I Timothy 6:11

1. What qualities should we seek after?

____

____

APPLICATION

IF'S

1. You fall and scrape your knee. What should you do?

____

____

____

____

It's time for your special night out with Mom and Dad. You've waited your turn for five months now. Unexpectedly, company drops in from out of town. Your special night will have to be postponed. What should you do?

____

____

____

____

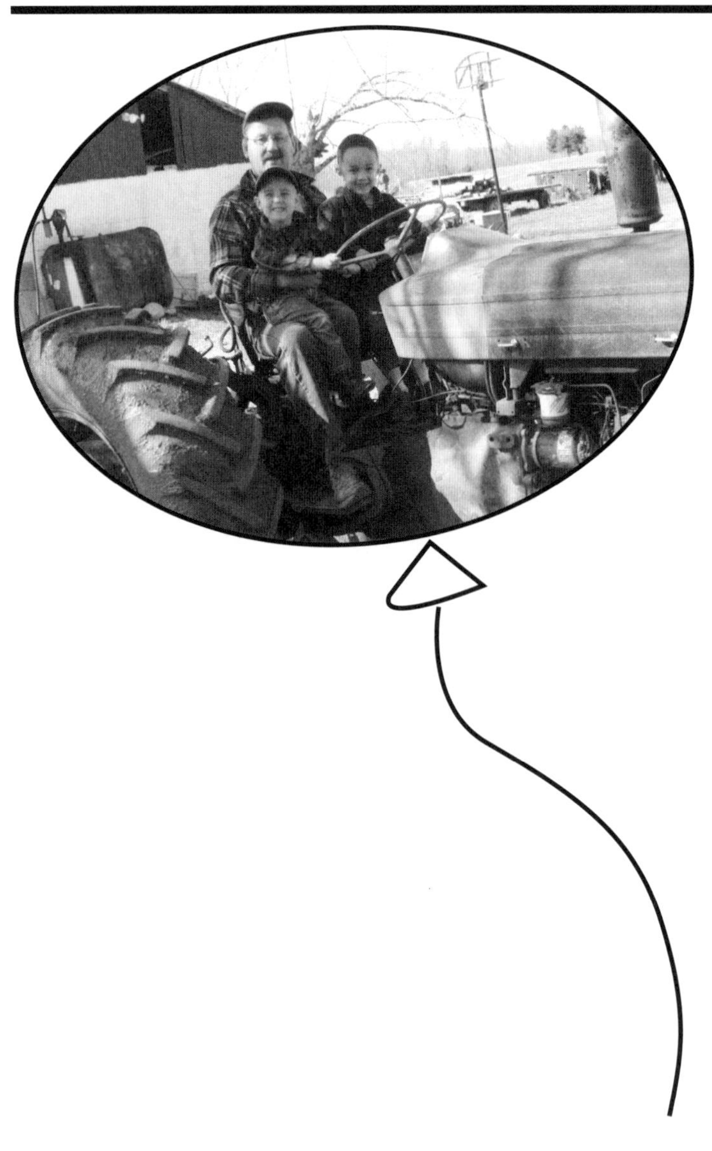

OBEDIENCE

DEFINITION

Doing what is expected of me cheerfully, immediately, and thoroughly

MEMORY VERSE

Children, obey your parents in all things: for this is well pleasing unto the Lord.

Colossians 3:20

Colossians 3:20

1. This verse tells you to obey your parents in ________________ things.
2. Why?

____

Ephesians 6:1

1. Why should you obey your parents?

____

____

Hebrews 13:17

1. You are told to obey ____________ that have the ________________ over you.
2. What responsibility is given to those who rule over others?

____

____

3. What would be unprofitable for you?

____

____

Ephesians 6:5

1. This verse is addressed to servants. We could apply it to employees as well. What are they told to do?

2. In what spirit should they obey?

3. When they obey earthly masters they should obey as

Acts 5:29

1. If an authority required us to do something clearly wrong, should we submit?

2. Whose authority is higher: God's, or that of another man?

Hebrews 5:8

1. How did Jesus learn obedience?

2. How should this affect you?

3. If Jesus learned obedience through suffering, should you be discouraged if things don't go your way?

4. What attitude should you have when your parents ask you to do something you don't want to do?

APPLICATION

IF'S

1. If you were having a great time playing a board game and Mom called you to do the dishes, what should you do?

____

____

____

____

2. If Mom told you to turn out the lights and go to sleep when you finished the chapter you were reading, but it ended at such an exciting place that you wanted to find out what happened, what should you do?

____

____

____

____

3. If Mom told you to put your clothes away and you stuffed them all under your bed, would you have obeyed?

____

____

____

____

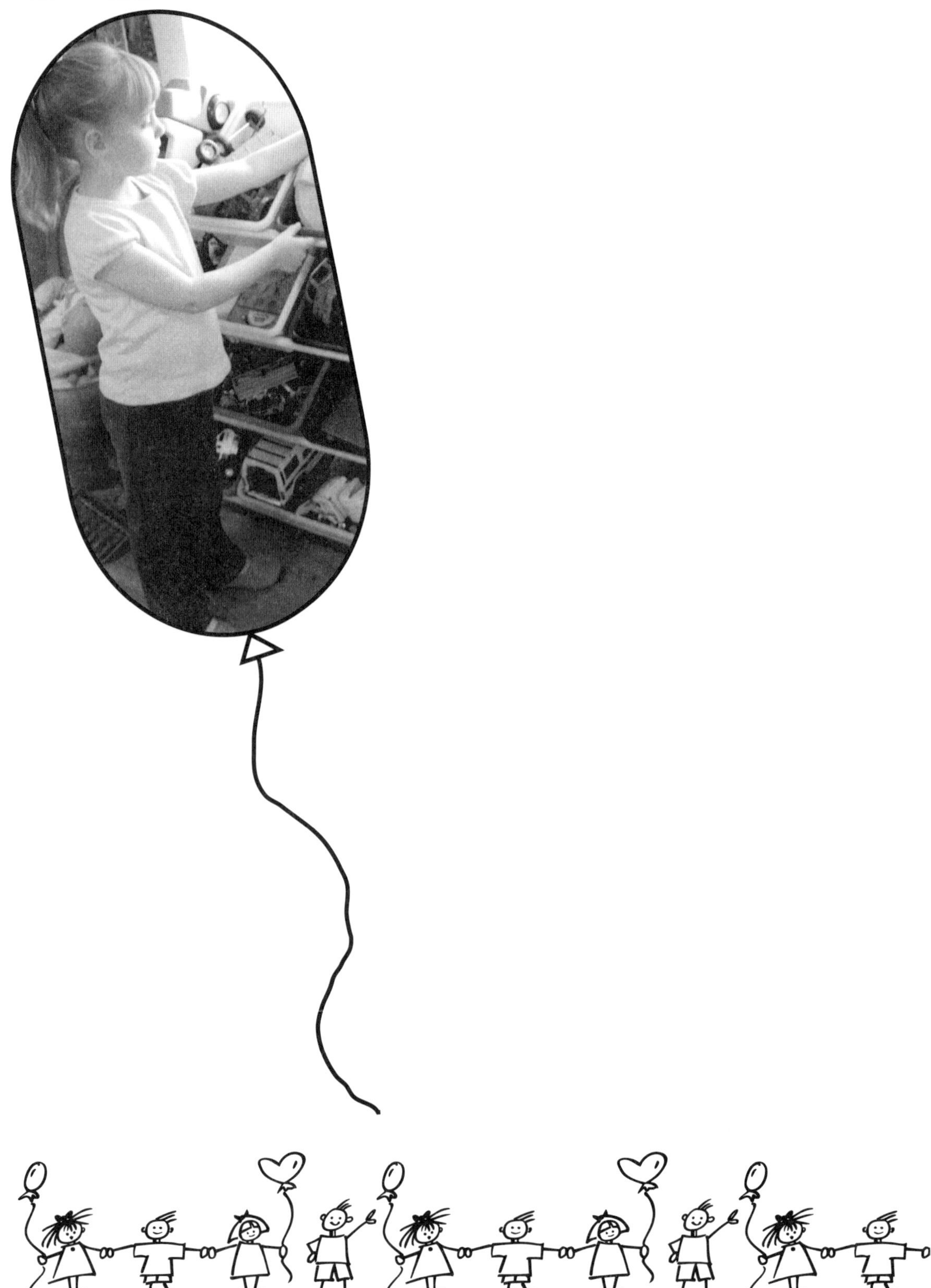

ORDERLINESS

DEFINITION

Managing my life and my belongings in order to reach maximum potential

MEMORY VERSE

Let all things be done decently and in order.

I Corinthians 14:40

Psalm 37:23

1. Who orders our steps?

____

____

____

Psalm 50:23

1. What does God give to one who orders his conversation (manner of life) rightly?

____

____

____

I Corinthians 14:40

1. How should we strive to do all things?

2. Another word for "decently" is "properly." How can you apply that to your everyday life?

I Corinthians 14:33

1. Did God design confusion or peace and order?

2. How is this reflected in creation?

APPLICATION

IF'S

1. Mom tells you to organize your room. How might you do this?

- Labels on storage containers (you can put pictures on containers if you have younger siblings who can't read).
- Make a place for everything, and label it.
- Make a game out of cleaning up with your younger siblings

2. You have certain chores to do on each day of the week. How might you remember what to do when?

____

____

____

____

PATIENCE

DEFINITION:

Waiting for God's timing with a happy heart

MEMORY VERSE:

Wherefore seeing we also are compassed about with so great a cloud of witnesses, let us lay aside every weight, and the sin which doth so easily beset us, and let us run with patience the race that is set before us.

Hebrews 12:1

James 5:10

1. From whom can we learn patience?

____

Romans 5:3

1. From what do we learn patience?

____

Colossians 1:10-12

1. How can we walk worthy of the Lord? What does patience have to do with this?

____

____

2. Where do we receive power to exercise patience?

____

3. What quality should we remember to be sure to exercise when experiencing tribulation? ____

James 1:3

1. If we correctly respond to problems that come into our life, what will be the fruit produced? ____________________

2. Should we be overanxious to get out of tough situations? ____________________

Hebrews 12:1-3

1. Who is watching us and cheering us on?

____

2. We need to beware that there is a sin which easily can beset us and guard against it. What sin is a big struggle in your life right now?

____

3. What quality must we use while running the race God has given us to run?

____

4. How can we learn from Jesus? Why did he endure the cross and shame?

____

____

Romans 12:12

1. What quality must we learn to exercise while undergoing tribulation? ____________________

2. There is a discipline we should exercise as well while undergoing tough circumstances. What is it? ____________________

1 Thessalonians 5:14

1. To whom are we to show patience? ____________________

1 Peter 2:20-22

1. How should we respond if we do right and suffer for it? ____________________

2. How does God view this when we learn to be patient in suffering? ____________________

____

3. Should we be surprised when this happens to us? ____________________

4. Who is our best example to follow when this happens to us?

____

APPLICATION

IF's

1. Your little brother loves to be doing what you are doing, but that means he tries to play with you, but breaks apart all your Lego creations. What should you do?

2. You plan to be helpful at church by trying to keep the little ones quiet while the adults talk. One adult comes over and reprimands you for getting them too excited. What should you do?

3. A family at church misunderstands your family's commitment to sit together as a family and says things that make you feel bad. What should you do?

PERSUASIVENESS

DEFINITION

Skillfully handling truth to lead others in a right path

MEMORY VERSE

And when they had appointed him a day, there came many to him into his lodging; to whom he expounded and testified the kingdom of God, persuading them concerning Jesus, both out of the law of Moses, and out of the prophets, from morning till evening.

Acts 28:23

1. For what purpose did Paul use persuasiveness?

____

2. How can you purpose to skillfully handle God's Word?

____

____

____

Acts 28:13

1. What was Paul accused of persuading men to do?

____

Matthew 27:20

People can persuade others to do something wrong as well. What instance of persuasion does this verse relate?

Acts 13:43

1. What did Paul and Barnabas persuade people to do?

Acts 26:28

1. What did Paul almost persuade King Agrippa to do?

Proverbs 25:15

1. What insight do we get into persuading a ruler?

Romans 8:38

1. Of what was Paul persuaded?

Romans 14:5

1. Of what should a person be fully persuaded?

APPLICATION

IF'S

1. You are burdened for the neighbor boy next door. You know he is not a Christian. How might you use persuasion to help him see his need more clearly?

____

____

____

____

2. Your older brother is considering breaking one of the family rules. How might you persuade him to obey?

____

____

____

____

Prudence

DEFINITION

Exercising caution in all situations;
foreseeing the consequences of my actions

MEMORY VERSE

A prudent man foreseeth the trouble and hides himself:
but the simple pass on and are punished.
Proverbs 22:3

1. Do the choices we make today affect us later?

____

2. Are there consequences for poor decisions?

____

3. Do we still suffer consequences for bad decisions if we realize they were bad?

____

Proverbs 13:16

1. Is a prudent man cautious with his words?

____

Proverbs 14:8

1. What is the wisdom of the prudent?

2. Is someone who acts now and thinks later considered prudent?

Proverbs 14:15

1. The simple believes everything he is told. What does the prudent do?

Proverbs 16:21

1. Who shall be called prudent?

APPLICATION

IF'S

1. Dad pays you for cleaning the car. Next month, he'll have you do it again, but there won't be any more paying jobs until then. What should you do with the money?

2. Grandma comes to visit and brings you two boxes of your favorite Drake's cakes. You only get them once a year. You're tempted to eat them all in a few days. What should you do?

PUNCTUALITY

DEFINITION

Being prompt in all commitments, honoring the time of others

MEMORY VERSE

Walk in wisdom toward them that are without, redeeming the time.

Colossians 4:5

1. Does our punctuality affect our testimony to others?

____

2. Could our being consistently late damage the name of Christ?

____

Ephesians 5:15-16

1. If we are wise, what will we do?

____

____

____

Psalm 90:12 (fill in the blanks)

"So teach us to ______________________________ our days, that we may ________________________________ our _________________________________ unto __________________________________."

Time is short. Our days are numbered. We need to remember this so we don't waste our time or the time of others.

APPLICATION

IF'S

1. If Mom calls you for dinner and you really want to finish the last paragraph of the chapter you're reading, what should you do?

2. Dad is calling everyone to come to family devotions. You need to run to the bathroom. What should you do?

3. Aunt Sue called to ask if you want to go to the zoo tomorrow. Mom says you may go if your chores are done on time. What should you do?

RESOURCEFULNESS

DEFINITION

Using things which others might discard
in a creative way

MEMORY VERSE

And whatsoever ye do, do it heartily, as to the Lord,
and not unto men; knowing that of the Lord
ye shall receive the reward of the inheritance:
for ye serve the Lord Christ.

Colossians 3:23-24

1. In everything we do, whom should we be aiming to please?

____

2. Who will ultimately reward us?

____

I Peter 4:19

1. In what should we not be weary?

____

2. Whom do we seek to please?

____

Ephesians 2:10

1. What were we created to do?

___

___

Colossians 1:16

1. By whom were all things created?

___

APPLICATION

IF'S

1. You want to give your Mom a birthday gift. You don't have any money available for that. What should you do?

2. You've been wanting a bird feeder to watch the birds in the yard. You don't have any money to buy a feeder. What could you do?

3. There is a pile of scrap lumber in the yard. You want to build a tree house, and Dad says you may use it. What could you do?

Respectfulness

DEFINITION

Treating others with honor and esteem

MEMORY VERSE

Let nothing be done through strife or vainglory; but in lowliness of mind let each esteem other better than themselves.

Philippians 2:3

You will never go wrong by treating others with honor. It communicates respect.

Ephesians 6:2

1. Who does this verse tell us to honor?

____

____

2. How will this benefit us?

____

____

____

2. What are some ways you show honor to your parents?

APPLICATION

IF'S

1. An older man rebukes you for squirming in church. What should you do?

2. You see a man in military uniform. How can you show him respect?

3. When someone speaks to you, where should you look to show respect?

4. When someone speaks to you but you are shy, what should you do?

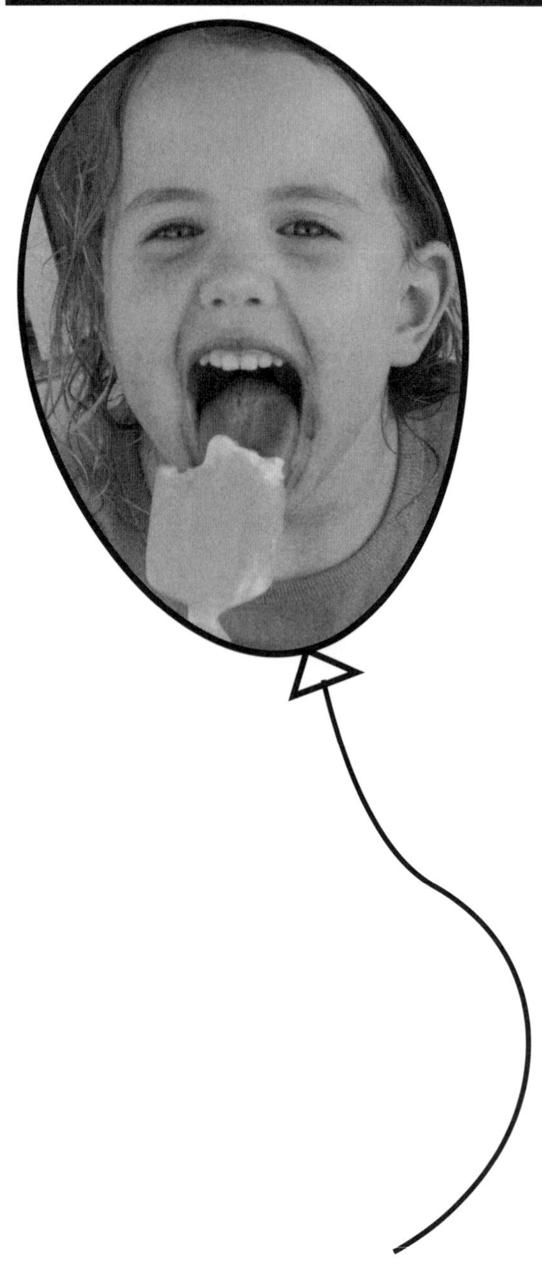

SELF-CONTROL

DEFINITION

Subjecting my own desire to the control of the Holy Spirit

MEMORY VERSE

He that hath no rule over his own spirit is like a city that is broken down and without walls.

Proverbs 25:28

In Bible days, cities had walls surrounding them for protection from enemies. The men of the city would defend the city from the top of the walls.

1. What would be the protection for a city with no walls?

___

___

___

2. What does this tell us of self-control?

___

___

Self-control is a guard over our own spirit. If we don't practice self-control, we are placing our spirit in danger.

Proverbs 16:32

1. What does this say of one who is slow to anger?

____

____

____

One who rules his spirit is better even than he that TAKES a city—not just defends it.

Proverbs 21:17

1. What does this verse tell us of one who loves pleasure?

____

____

____

APPLICATION

IF'S

1. You are eating chocolate cake with chocolate icing for dessert. There is lots to spare. You'd like to have another slice. What should you do?

____

____

____

____

2. The neighbor boy purposely broke your fishing pole and then laughed about it. You feel like slugging him. What should you do?

____

____

____

____

3. You have a new computer game. It is so much fun you can't stop playing! You have chores and reading to do, but you'd like to play another round. What should you do?

____

____

____

____

SENSITIVITY

DEFINITION

The ability to put yourself in another's shoes and trying to see life from his point of view

MEMORY VERSE

Put on therefore, as the elect of God, holy and beloved, bowels of mercies, kindness, humbleness of mind, meekness, long-suffering; forbearing one another…

Colossians 3:12-13a

1. Think of someone who treated you with sensitivity sometime when you were upset.

____

2. What does it mean to forbear another?

____

____

____

Philippians 2:1-3

1. How can we best comfort another?

____

____

____

2. Fill in the blanks:

"Fulfill ye my ______________, that ye be __________________________________,
having the same _________________, being of __________ ____________________,
of ___________ ________________. Let ________________________ be done
through __________________________ or _____________________________;
but in _____________________________ of ____________________, let each
_______________________ ____________________ _____________________ than
themselves."

3. How can you learn to be of one mind with someone else?

____

____

____

____

4. Do you ever think what it would be like to be another person when something hard happens to him? By trying to feel how he must feel, you are humbling yourself and can best comfort him.

____

____

____

____

APPLICATION

IF'S

1. The neighbor boy just got a new bike for his birthday. Excitedly, he calls to you to "watch this!" Jumping on his bike, he gets up speed and promptly crashes into the garage, skinning his knees and elbows. What should you do?

____

____

____

____

2. Mom and Dad got their dog on their honeymoon. They've now had her 14 years and she just died from old age. Mom is crying. What should you do?

____

____

____

____

3. Your friend's mom just had a miscarriage. Your friend was REALLY excited about getting a new little sister. They are very upset. What should you do?

____

____

____

____

THOROUGHNESS

DEFINITION

Bringing to completion each task I do with excellence

MEMORY VERSE

Better is the end of a thing than the beginning thereof:
and the patient in spirit is better than the proud in spirit.

Ecclesiastes 7:8

It is easy and exciting to start a project, but as time goes on, sometimes we tire of it and want to quit.

1. What does this verse say is better than starting a project?

____

____

____

When we begin a project, we should determine to bring it to completion.

1 Corinthians 10:31

1. This verse tells us to do all we do for whom?

____

2. Fill in the blanks:

"Whether therefore ye _____________________ or ___________________________, or _____________________________ ye do, do ___________ to the __________________ of ______________."

Colossians 3:17

1. Again, for whom should we do our best?

____

____

THOROUGHNESS

APPLICATION

IF'S

1. You tell your mom you're going to make her a clay nativity. The pieces are so intricate, it keeps breaking. What should you do?

2. You've had company over and your room is extra messy. Mom tells you if you pick it up really well she's going to reward you with ice cream at Coldstone's. About half-way through, you're tempted to stuff the rest in the closet. What should you do?

3. You're preparing a report on mammals. You're supposed to use three sources. There are so many other things you'd like to do that you're tempted to use only one source and get it finished. What should you do?

TOLERANCE

DEFINITION

Giving others room to grow at different rates
as God leads them

MEMORY VERSE

But when ye sin so against the brethren, and wound their weak conscience, ye sin against Christ. Wherefore, if meat make my brother to offend, I will eat no meat while the world standeth, lest I make my brother to offend.

1 Corinthians 8:12-13

This verse refers to meat that was offered to idols. Some felt that it was wrong to buy that meat because it had been used in idolatry. Others felt it was a wise use of money (it was cheaper than other meat), as they didn't believe in idols anyway.

1. What is Paul's instruction here?

____

____

____

2. What is more important than whether or not they ate the meat?

____

____

Sometimes we need to limit ourselves so as not to offend others. We must realize God deals with different individuals at different times, and the most important thing is people's spiritual condition.

2 Corinthians 6:3

1. What does this verse tell us?

___

___

___

Matthew 18:7

2. What caution does this verse give us?

___

___

___

APPLICATION

IF'S

We had a rule for our children that they couldn't tell a younger brother or sister that their schoolwork was "EASY." It was easy for them now, but not when they were the age of the younger sibling. To do so would make them feel inferior or slow.

1. You see your brother struggling with his multiplication tables and you find them easy. What should you do?

____

____

____

____

2. Your cousins believe in Santa Claus but you don't. What should you do?

____

____

____

____

2. You hear your friends listening to music that is off-limits at your house, what should you do?

____

____

____

____

To be tolerant doesn't mean you have to lower your standards or tell people whatever they think is fine. It does mean that you treat them kindly, using discretion, and if they sincerely ask why you do things differently, then give them an honest explanation.

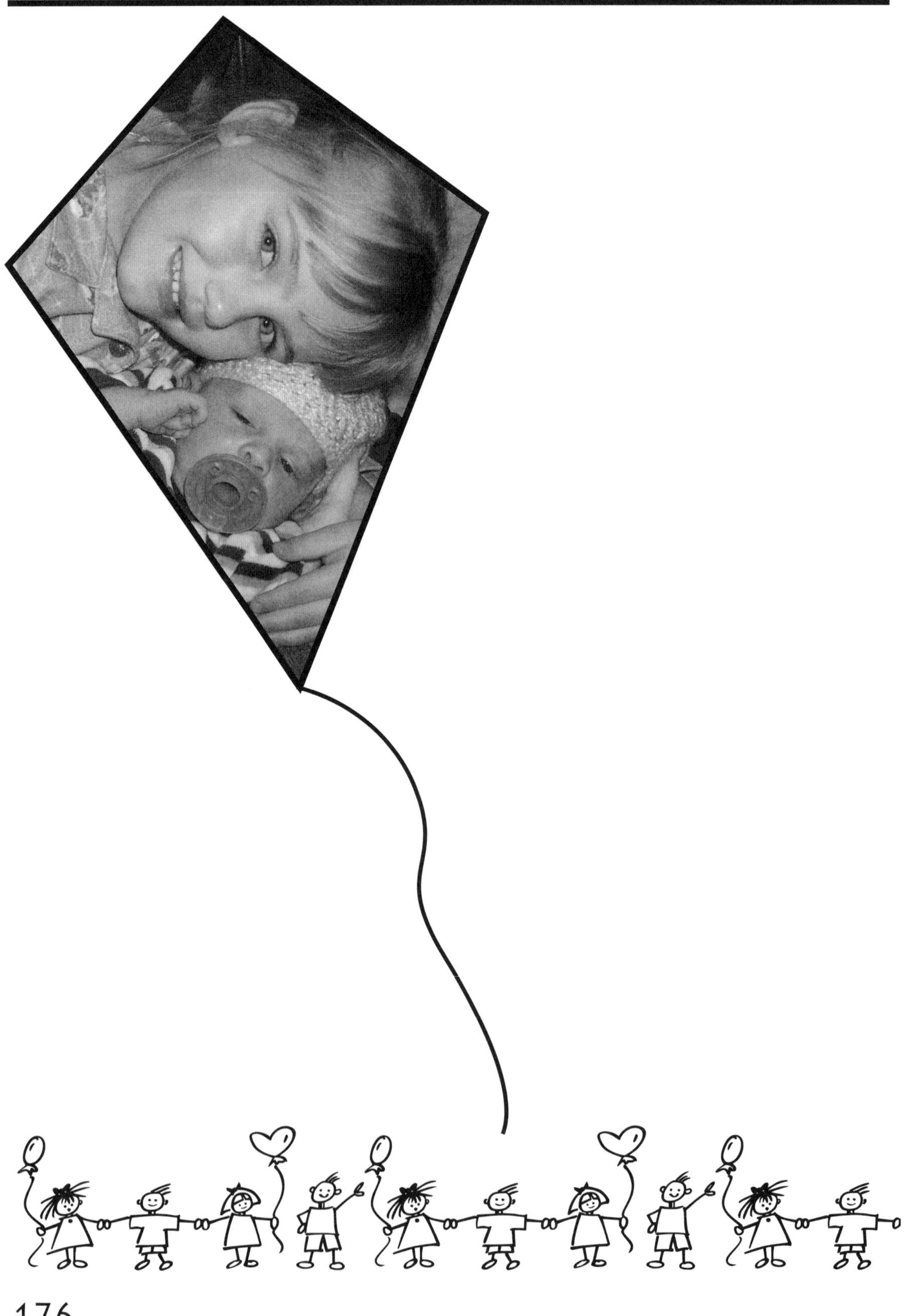

TRUTHFULNESS

DEFINITION

Trustworthiness by accurately stating the facts

MEMORY VERSE

Hear; for I will speak of excellent things; and the opening of my lips shall be right things. For my mouth shall speak truth; and wickedness is an abomination to my lips.

Proverbs 8:6-7

1. What type of words should we purpose to speak?

____

2. What does this verse tell us about speaking lies?

____

Proverbs 12:19

1. For how long is truth established?

____

Proverbs 12:22

1. What does God delight in?

____

Proverbs 8:7

1. What shall we purpose to speak?

____

Proverbs 23:23

1. How important is truth?

____

____

2. What should be our response and commitment to truth?

____

____

____

Ephesians 4:25

1. What shall we speak of with our neighbor?

____

Ephesians 6:14

1. What part of the armor of God should we "girt about our loins"?

____

____

APPLICATION

IF'S

1. You are watching the baby. He slipped out of your arms and fell. You are tempted to just tell Mom he pulled himself up and lost his balance. What should you do?

2. Mom asks if you took our vitamins. You don't like taking vitamins and would rather not. What should you do?

3. You hear of something that another person is suspected of having done wrong. You'd love to tell your friend what you know. What should you do?

VIRTUE

DEFINITION

Maintaining moral excellence and setting godly standards

MEMORY VERSE

And beside this, giving all diligence, add to your faith virtue, and to virtue knowledge.

2 Peter 1:5

Philippians 4:8

1. Write this list of things we should intentionally focus our mind on:

"Finally, brethren, whatsoever things are ___________________, whatsoever things are ____________________________, whatsoever things are ______________________, whatsoever things are _______________________________, whatsoever things are _____________________________________, whatsoever things are of ____________ ________________, if there be any _______________________, and if there be any ____________________, think on these things."

By thinking on these things, we can add to our faith.

2 Peter 1:3

1. To what has God called us?

____

2. What has his divine power given to us?

____

____

Proverbs 12:4

1. What is a virtuous woman to her husband?

____

____

Proverbs 31:10

1. What is the worth of a virtuous woman?

____

____

____

APPLICATION

IF'S

1. When something troubles us and we keep thinking about it, what should we do?

____

____

____

____

2. How can we control our thoughts?

____

____

____

____

3. Does God's Word actually change our thoughts?

____

____

____

____

Isaiah 55:8-9 (fill in the blanks):

"For my ____________________ are not your ________________, neither are your ________________ my ________________, saith the Lord. For as the ____________________ are higher than the ________________, so are my ________________ higher than your ________________, and my ____________________ than your thoughts."

If we will memorize and meditate on (think about) God's Word, wc will begin to exchange our earthly thoughts for God's thoughts.

WISDOM

DEFINITION

Learning to see life from God's point of view

MEMORY VERSE

So teach us to number our days,
that we may apply our hearts unto wisdom.
Psalm 90:12

Proverbs 1:5

1. What does this verse tell us the wise man does?

____

____

Proverbs 9:8

1. How does a wise person respond to rebuke?

____

____

This would be wise to remember the next time your parents rebuke you.

Proverbs 9:9

1. Does a wise person like to learn?

____

Proverbs 10:1

1. If you are wise, how does that affect your dad?

___

___

Proverbs 13:1

1. How does a wise son respond to his father's instruction?

___

___

Proverbs 13:20

1. What type of friends does a wise person choose?

___

___

Proverbs 16:23

1. Does a wise person control his words?

___

___

APPLICATION

IF'S

1. Your dad tells you how to improve your table manners. How should you respond?

2. A group of boys at church seem to be laughing at the wrong things and whispering among themselves. Should you try to enter their circle of friendship?

3. Think of something you did that showed wisdom. How did it make your dad feel?

4. Aunt Margaret asks how you like her soup. Should you tell her it was awful? How could you choose your words more carefully?

RESOURCES AVAILABLE FROM THE LEARNING PARENT

CHARACTER CONCEPTS FOR PRESCHOOLERS • BASIC CURRICULUM

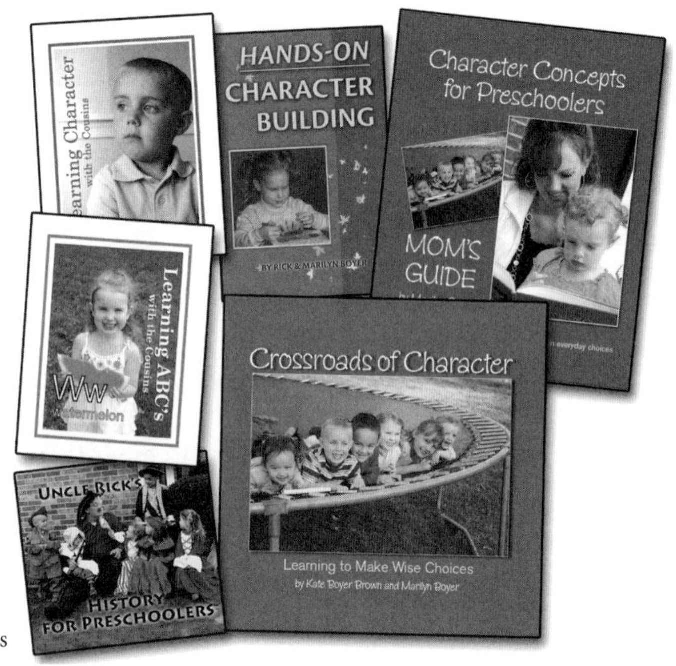

The most important thing you can teach your preschooler is character. *Character Concepts for Preschoolers* provides 36 weeks of lessons for preschoolers, teaching them, first and foremost, character and Scripture, which lays the foundation for all other learning. This curriculum teaches children the meaning of 12 character qualities, and guides them in using wisdom to apply them in everyday life. They are also given an appropriate Scripture to learn, so they can find out what God has to say about this character quality.This curriculum will guide you in implementing practical projects to help your child internalize what he is learning. *Hands-on Character Building* is one of the tools we provide along with instructions for when and how to use it. Your child will learn his ABC's with the *Learning ABC's with the Cousins* colorful set of flashcards.

Also included in this curriculum are craft and nature projects, season-appropriate where applicable. There are suggestions for science units and recipes are given to make with your child. Suggestions are made for a field trip destination along the lines of what they've been learning.It is very adaptable to your schedule and is appropriate for use with older children as well.

CHARACTER CONCEPTS FOR PRESCHOOLERS • COMPLETE CURRICULUM

This set includes our brand new *Character Concepts for Preschoolers* Curriculum along with the Character Concepts for Preschoolers Recommended Resource Pack—10 items in all.

Character Concepts for Preschoolers · Science Collection

This hardcover collection provides one book for each of the 12 units studied during the year. It is colorfully illustrated and gives just enough information to capture a preschooler's interest.

Character Concepts for Preschoolers · Resource Pack

This package includes resources for additional Scripture memory, Bible doctrine, and academic resources for the preschool year. Included in this pack are the following books, which may also be purchased individually if you already own some of the pieces:

Leading Little Ones to God—teaches Bible doctrine

Making Wise Choices Flashcard set—Includes 3 sets of flashcards for memorization: *Character Quality, Proverbs,* and *If/When,* which teaches children Scripture useful for making everyday decisions.

Proverbs for Preschoolers—a beginning letter skills book.

Christian Liberty Press Workbook—teaches letter and number recognition, shapes, colors, opposites, sizes, matching, patterns, and more!

On My Own Biographies

I can't tell you how delighted I was to find early readers about true American heroes—books well worth reading. Kasey, at age five was captivated to listen to Tuck, her older brother, as he was learning to read! We recently made an amazing discovery! My daughter-in-law, Kari, was looking for history hero stories for Cassidy, who was three years old. I loaned her a set of these readers and Cass was captivated by them! So, read them to your preschoolers, teach your beginning readers to read with them, and use them all the way up to third grade level. If your child wants to read the story again and again (which mine did), and then they progress to learning to read on their own, it can only benefit them to be familiar with the story. That is the process by which my oldest son taught himself to read.

Proverbs People Collection

Proverbs People Collection features *Proverbs People workbooks I and II,* our most popular products for children aged seven to twelve. Your 7-12 year olds will learn how to relate to people God's way as they study major character types in the book of Wisdom in practical detail.

In addition, it includes *Proverbs People* flashcards providing two Bible verses for each character type presented in the *Proverbs People* workbooks. The collection also features the 5-cd set, *Uncle Rick Reads the Proverbs.* Pop one of these cd's in at naptime, bedtime or travel time and your children will hear Uncle Rick read and explain the entire book of Proverbs. They will memorize God's word effortlessly and can go to sleep each night meditating on its mighty truth. Help your child experience the power of Scripture through character study and reinforced listening as well!

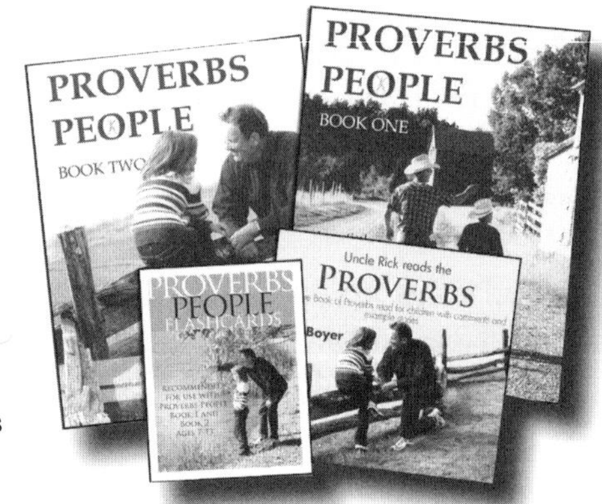

Teach your 7-12 year olds how to relate to people God's way! In these two big workbooks, every major character type in the book of Wisdom is studied in practical detail. **Teach social and spiritual skills to your child by precept, not by chance!**

Uncle Rick Reads • Audiobooks

Let Uncle Rick teach your preschooler history in the form of true stories of heroes from America's past. It's a fun way to learn and your children can learn even while playing or riding in the car. Uncle Rick reads stories from books written in the 1800's when they taught character qualities like honesty and kindness. Uncle Rick makes his character comments along the way.

There are lots of audiobooks to choose from at www.thelearningparent.com.

Growing in Wisdom Character Studies

This study is based on the popular handout *Identifying and Dealing with Offenses* by Marilyn Boyer. Your child will learn 32 types of negative behavior and their Biblical consequences. Through insights learned from God's Word, your child will be guided in making an intentional decision to choose positive, godly character in their day to day life. God has the answer for turning our negative natural tendencies into choices which reflect the character of Jesus Christ.

Growing in Wisdom Flashcards is a set of 32 flashcards to be used in coordination with *Growing in Wisdom Character Studies.* 32 flashcards are provided to help children learn the positive quality which is the opposite of the negative trait demonstrated. On the back side of the card is the Scripture verse which addresses the problem with its reference and also an insight to be gleaned from Scripture directed at helping your child to make a wise practical decision.

Appropriate for ages 7-14. 201pages.

RESOURCES AVAILABLE FROM THE LEARNING PARENT

THE BOYER LIBRARY

Get a big dose of encouragement when you buy all six books in the Boyer library! Books include: *Parenting from the Heart, The Hands-on Dad, Yes, They're All Ours, Home Educating with Confidence, Fun Projects for Hands-on Character Building,* and *The Socialization Trap.* If you have one of the collection already, consider giving it away as a gift!

A FEW ENDORSEMENTS . . .

Parenting from the Heart
"Reading *Parenting From the Heart* is like a friendly visit at the kitchen table over a steaming cup of tea with a godly older sister in the Lord, gleaning from her many years of experience and gentle wisdom. How I wish Marilyn had written this book when my oldest were little! Be prepared to receive an encouraging hug—you just supply the cup of tea!" —Tracy Klicka, nationally known home school speaker and writer, wife of Chris Klicka, senior counsel, Home School Legal Defense Association

The Socialization Trap
"I have just completed your book *The Socialization Trap.* Thank you so much for your shared wisdom and insights. I think every parent should have to read this book." —a mom from California

The Hands-on Dad
"My husband is not a reader, but he just loves Rick Boyer's writing! Rick has a gift for making people feel comfortable. He's very approachable. Thanks a million!" —a mom from South Carolina

These resources can be purchased at www.thelearningparent.com